Food Safety

CHRISTINE TAYLOR-BUTLER

Children's Press®
An Imprint of Scholastic Inc.
New York Toronto London Auckland Sydney
Mexico City New Delhi Hong Kong
Danbury, Connecticut

Content Consultant
Lawrence J. Cheskin, M.D., F.A.C.P.
Associate Professor,
Johns Hopkins Bloomberg School of Public Health
The Johns Hopkins University
Baltimore, Maryland

Library of Congress Cataloging-in-Publication Data

Taylor-Butler, Christine.
  Food safety / by Christine Taylor-Butler.
        p. cm. -- (A true book)
  Includes index.
      ISBN-13: 978-0-531-16860-8 (lib. bdg.)
               978-0-531-20734-5 (pbk.)
      ISBN-10: 0-531-16860-3 (lib. bdg.)
               0-531-20734-X (pbk.)
  1. Food handling--Safety measures--Juvenile literature. 2. Food
poisoning--Juvenile literature. I. Title. II. Series.

  TX537.T39 2008
  363.19'262--dc22   2007036014

Produced by Weldon Owen Education Inc.

1 2 3 4 5 6 7 8 9 10 R 17 16 15 14 13 12 11 10 09 08

Find the Truth!

Everything you are about to read is true *except* for one of the sentences on this page.

Which one is **TRUE**?

T or F At Thanksgiving, there is a hotline that explains how to cook a turkey safely.

T or F All bacteria are bad for your body.

Find the answers in this book.

Contents

THE **BIG** TRUTH!

Refrigerator Safety

Eggs with cracks are unsafe to eat.

Leaving some foods uncovered and unchilled at picnics and barbecues can be a food-safety risk.

CHAPTER 1

What's for Lunch?

An important food-safety rule is to keep hot food hot and cold food cold.

Your family is having a barbecue in the park. There is coleslaw, cold chicken, and fruit salad. Hamburgers and hot dogs are cooking on the grill. But a softball game is about to start. When you finally eat your lunch, your food has been out in the sun for a while. You're so hungry that you forget to wash your hands before eating.

If you have food poisoning, you may run a fever.

The next morning, you wake up feeling ill.
Your head hurts. You have stomach cramps.
You keep running to the bathroom. Your mother
takes your temperature. She says that you have
a fever. What's going on?

You have food poisoning. Remember the warm
weather and the softball game? Your lunch was
left too long in the sun before you ate it. When
you ate lunch, you also ate some harmful
bacteria. They made you sick.

If cooked food is left at room temperature for more than two hours, it may be unsafe to eat.

Barbecue Food Safety

It is important to know which foods are safe to eat after being unchilled at a barbecue for two hours. Some foods should be thrown out.

Safe

Unsafe

Bread

Coleslaw

Fruit salad

Hamburger

Hotdog

Muffin

Mustard

Cream pie

Food poisoning is a common illness. It is caused by tiny **microbes**, such as bacteria, in food. Many people don't even know when they get food poisoning. They recover very quickly. But some people get very sick. They have to go to the hospital. Some people even die from it.

Listeria (lihs-TIHR-ee-uh) bacteria can cause food poisoning. They can be found in raw foods. Heating and cooking food properly can kill *Listeria*. Washing foods with warm water can also kill them.

Moldy Food

Keeping food safe helps keep us safe. Food spoils if it is not preserved. Different foods take different amounts of time to spoil. Fruit can be kept fresh for weeks at room temperature. Nuts can last for months. Some foods go bad in a few days. In hotter weather, food spoils more quickly. Sometimes it is difficult to tell that food contains harmful microbes. However, there can be obvious signs. Microbes such as **mold** change the flavor and smell of foods. Moldy foods should be thrown away. Never taste food to find out whether it is safe.

Some people believe it is not
safe to eat foods that have
been sprayed with chemicals.
Supermarkets usually stock
many spray-free foods.

CHAPTER 2

What Is Food Safety?

Food comes from many different places. It goes through many inspections. These make sure that it is safe to eat before it gets to the supermarket.

Some forms of poisoning may be caused by chemicals, such as lead. Many people now eat **organic** foods. Farmers who grow organic crops do not use chemical **pesticides** on their produce.

Fruit skins may contain harmful chemicals from pesticides.

The Government at Work

The U.S. government has several departments that work to keep your food supply as safe as possible. Inspectors check food before it gets to the grocery store. They look at each food's appearance and smell. They check its storage, labeling, handling, and cleanliness.

The United States buys some of its food from other countries. Scientists work with international groups, such as the World Health Organization, to make sure that the food bought from other countries is safe.

An inspector checks produce as it arrives in the United States.

14

The USDA has a poultry hotline. People can phone it at Thanksgiving. They can ask questions about how to cook and store a turkey safely.

The Food Safety and Inspection Service (FSIS) is part of the U.S. Department of Agriculture (USDA). The FSIS makes sure that the meat, poultry, and eggs you buy are safe to eat. It makes rules about packaging and about the safety information that is printed on food labels.

The Food and Drug Administration (FDA) looks after the public health of people in the United States. Part of that job includes making safety rules for seafood, fruits, vegetables, and other foods.

The Environmental Protection Agency (EPA) helps make sure your drinking water is safe. It tests the water in streams and lakes for harmful bacteria.

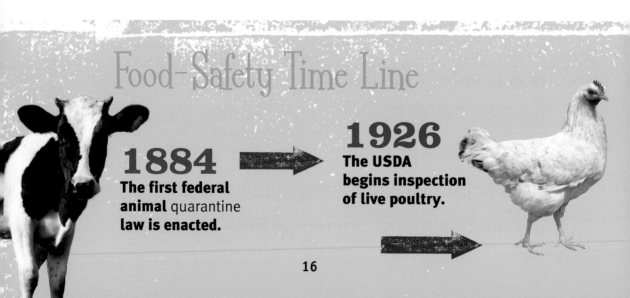

Food-Safety Time Line

1884
The first federal
animal quarantine
law is enacted.

1926
The USDA
begins inspection
of live poultry.

Your local city or county health department has inspectors too. They make sure the food you eat is handled correctly in stores and restaurants. They inspect school cafeterias too. They check the kitchens. They ensure that the workers practice good hygiene. Workers should wash their hands before preparing or serving food. Only healthy workers should handle food. They should also wear clean clothes.

1939
The first grading standards are issued by the USDA. They are for a frozen product (peas).

1970
The Egg Products Inspection Act is passed.

Here a researcher is working on food safety. He has taken samples from a turkey to see what bacteria are living on it. He has grown the bacteria on petri dishes.

CHAPTER 3

Bacteria Everywhere

 There are thousands of kinds of bacteria.

Bacteria are found in your body. They are found in the air, water, and soil. They are on your food. Bacteria are one-celled microorganisms. These tiny living things can be seen only with a microscope. Bacteria need food and moisture. Most also need warm temperatures.

Bacteria help ripen cheese. Swiss cheese ripens for several months.

The holes in Swiss cheese are made from bacteria. The bacteria give off carbon dioxide gas as they digest food. The gas makes air pockets in the cheese.

Helpful Bacteria

Some bacteria are helpful. Many bacteria that live in the body's intestine help digest food. They also produce vitamin K. The bacteria in some yogurt can help with digestion. Some bacteria are even used to make medicines.

Harmful Bacteria

Many kinds of bacteria can make you sick. Bacteria found in our food can multiply very quickly. This is the case if the food has been kept at a warm temperature or not handled properly. Harmful bacteria often produce toxins (poisons). They destroy healthy cells.

Canning helps preserve foods. Botulism is a kind of food poisoning. It can be fatal. Bacteria that cause botulism can live in canned food that has not been sterilized properly.

Botulinum bacteria are found in soil. They can survive in boiling water for hours!

Salmonella Bacteria

Salmonella (sal-muh-NELL-uh) bacteria can harm you. They can **contaminate** food and water. Salmonellosis is the most common cause of food poisoning. The rod-shaped bacteria that cause it can be found in poultry, eggs, and milk. You can avoid spreading *Salmonella* bacteria by cooking food properly. You should also wash your hands after going to the bathroom and after touching pets.

Salmonella bacteria can exist on the shell of an egg.

Pulsed light is a method of food preservation. These eggs are receiving pulsed light. The light kills bacteria in and on the eggs.

Restaurant workers often wear gloves. This prevents the transfer of bacteria from their skin to the food.

Staph Bacteria

Staphylococcus (staf-uh-loh-KAHK-uhss) *aureus* bacteria are round microorganisms. They are commonly found on our skin and in our noses. If the bacteria get into our food, they may make us sick. If they do, they usually cause **diarrhea** and vomiting. This can occur just a few hours after the contaminated food has been eaten.

E. Coli Bacteria

Escherichia (ehsh-uh-RIHK-ee-uh) *coli* (*E. coli*) bacteria are found in the intestines of humans and animals. Most types of *E. coli* are harmless. Some are even helpful. However, some create toxins that force the intestine to make extra fluids. This causes diarrhea. It can take up to three weeks to recover if you get sick from *E. coli*.

Washing hands after going to the bathroom is a good way to prevent *E. coli* bacteria from spreading.

Food can be contaminated with *E. coli* if it is washed with unclean water. In 2006, many people throughout the United States got sick from eating raw spinach. Scientists believe the spinach was grown using water contaminated by a nearby animal farm. The FDA issued a public warning.

Raw spinach is usually safe to eat. However, in 2006, this spinach product was recalled.

Clean It

A refrigerator slows down bacterial growth. However, it does not stop it. That is why it is important to wash the fridge regularly. Use hot, soapy water. If you spill food, then wipe it up right away.

Throw It

Remember not to keep food in the refrigerator for too long. Leftovers can sometimes keep for three to four days. Fresh poultry lasts only about two days.

Don't Cram It

It is important not to overload the refrigerator. To keep it cool and the food safe, air needs to circulate. Use the different shelves and compartments to keep different foods separated. Don't store perishable foods in the door. Try to keep the door closed as much as possible.

Refrigerator Safety

Some foods, such as meat and milk, can go bad in only a few hours if they are not chilled or stored in a refrigerator. It is important to refrigerate food promptly. Food can still be hot when it goes into the refrigerator. A few basic "rules" will help you keep food safe there. The main rule is "keep it cool."

Chill It

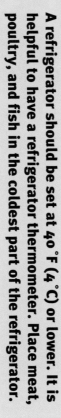

A refrigerator should be set at 40° F (4°C) or lower. It is helpful to have a refrigerator thermometer. Place meat, poultry, and fish in the coldest part of the refrigerator.

27

Many people have to drink the same water they use for washing.

CHAPTER 4

Around the World

 More than two billion people worldwide are infected with microbes from unsafe food or water.

When you take a drink of water, or wash your fruits and vegetables under the faucet, you take for granted that the water is safe to use. But in many countries, people have to take extra care when drinking water. It may be contaminated with bacteria such as *E. coli* from human or animal waste.

Many U.S. children drink milk at home and at school. The USDA requires milk to be heated and quickly cooled to kill any bacteria or viruses. This is called **pasteurization**. But children in many parts of the world drink raw milk. They may drink it straight from the cow or goat. They are at risk of food poisoning from bacteria in the milk.

In 1864, French scientist Louis Pasteur developed pasteurization. He first used it to keep microbes from turning wine bitter.

Milk is pasteurized at a milk processing plant. Refrigerated tankers transport milk to the plant. The temperature inside the tanker is about 40 °F (4 °C) This helps prevent bacteria from growing.

Manufacturers in the United States also pasteurize other foods. These include eggs and orange juice. However, it is still a good idea not to eat meals containing raw eggs. *Salmonella* bacteria can be in the yolk, the egg white, and even the eggshell. Homemade salad dressings and ice cream may contain raw eggs too.

If you're making cookies, remember not to lick the spoon. The uncooked cookie dough may contain raw eggs.

31

Unwashed fruits and vegetables may be unsafe to eat. Ensure that you wash them with warm water. They may have come into contact with harmful bacteria in the soil.

CHAPTER 5

Fighting Bacteria

The U.S. government, food manufacturers, and consumer groups have joined together to run a food-safety campaign. It is called Fight BAC! The campaign suggests four simple steps to help reduce the risk of getting food poisoning. These are: Clean, Separate, Cook, and Chill.

Fight BAC! stands for "fight bacteria."

Clean

Washing your hands is one of the most important things you can do to keep your food safe. Use soap and warm, running water. Wash your hands for at least 20 seconds.

Remember to wash your hands before you prepare food and eat. You may have picked up some bacteria that could make you sick.

Wash Your Hands ...

- **Before handling food**

- **After handling food**

- **After blowing your nose, coughing, or sneezing**

- **After using the bathroom**

- **After playing outside**

- **After touching a pet**

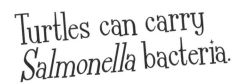

Turtles can carry *Salmonella* bacteria.

You should replace
worn cutting boards.
It can be difficult
to keep them clean.

Chopping boards, utensils, and countertops should be cleaned. Use hot water and detergents or **disinfectant** cleansers. Wash chopping boards before and after working with raw meat, poultry, eggs, and seafood. This helps avoid cross-contamination. Washing sponges and dish towels in the hot cycle of the washing machine is also a good idea.

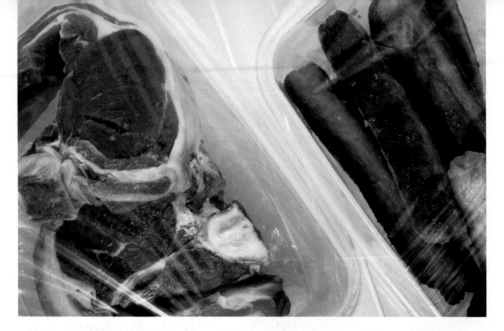

Store cooked and raw foods separately. Use containers, plastic bags, or plastic wrap. Place raw meats at the bottom of the refrigerator.

Separate

Bacteria can spread from one food to another very easily. It is important to keep raw meat, poultry, eggs, and seafood from coming into contact with ready-to-eat foods, such as fruits and vegetables.

If you are helping prepare a meal, don't use the same chopping board for salad and bread that you use for meat. Be sure that juices from raw meat don't drip onto other foods in the refrigerator.

Cook

Cooking foods until they reach a high enough internal temperature will kill most bacteria. There is a recommended range of temperatures for cooking different foods safely. It ranges from about 145 °F (63 °C) for fish to 180 °F (82 °C) for turkey. If you are reheating leftovers, make sure they get really hot too. They need to reach 165 °F (74 °C) to be safe. A food thermometer can be used to measure the temperature.

Ground beef
160 °F (71 °C)

Chicken
165 °F (74 °C)

Pork
160 °F (71 °C)

If you are microwaving food, follow the cooking instructions on the package.

Chill

Many bacteria cannot grow in a cold environment. Put cooked food in the refrigerator as soon as you can. Frozen food should be defrosted in the refrigerator, not on the countertop. This prevents it from getting too warm. There are ideal temperatures for chilling and cooking food. There is a temperature danger zone in which bacteria multiply quickly.

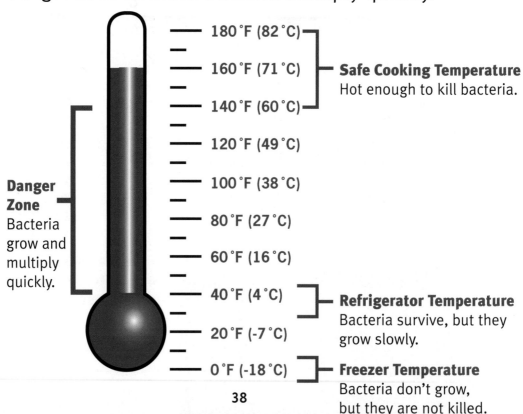

180°F (82°C)
160°F (71°C) — **Safe Cooking Temperature** Hot enough to kill bacteria.
140°F (60°C)
120°F (49°C)
100°F (38°C)
80°F (27°C)
60°F (16°C)
40°F (4°C) — **Refrigerator Temperature** Bacteria survive, but they grow slowly.
20°F (-7°C)
0°F (-18°C) — **Freezer Temperature** Bacteria don't grow, but they are not killed.

Danger Zone Bacteria grow and multiply quickly.

An insulated cooler with icepacks is a safe way to take food to outdoor events. Keep the lid closed as much as you can. Place the cooler in the shade.

39

Use-By Dates

Many packaged foods show a sell-by or a use-by date on their label. To be sure the food is safe, you should buy the food before the sell-by date. You need to eat it before the use-by date. The use-by date is sometimes called the best-before date. The label may also have instructions about how to safely prepare the food. Different manufacturers have different systems of showing information on food labels.

What Do You Do If You Get Sick?

If you think you have food poisoning, you may need to be treated by a doctor. You will be asked to list the foods you have eaten recently. That will help the doctor find out what made you sick. Most cases of food poisoning get better without medicine. A stomachache will probably go away by itself.

If you are vomiting or have diarrhea, get plenty of rest. Drink lots of fluids too. Avoid drinks with sugar or caffeine, such as sodas. It is also very important to wash your hands thoroughly after you go to the bathroom. This will help prevent other people from getting sick.

A child's body is made up of about 75 percent water.

Safe Again

When you begin to feel better, you can eat a little plain food. Stick to rice, bread, and potatoes. Lean meats, yogurt, fruits, and vegetables are also good. Stay clear of fatty or sugary foods. Foods such as oatmeal, carrots, and apples are high in soluble fiber. They help restore the bacteria that help your digestion. When you are well again, you will be able to practice the four steps for safe food handling. You can become an expert on food safety. Remember— when in doubt, throw it out! ★

Number of kinds of *Staph* bacteria: About 30

Number of kinds of *Salmonella* bacteria: About 2,300

Temperature setting for freezer: 0 °F (-18 °C)

Number of food-borne illnesses each year in the United States: About 76 million

Average temperature needed to kill bacteria: 160 °F (71 °C)

Year New York and Chicago first required milk to be pasteurized: 1908

Ideal temperature for bacteria to grow: 98.6 °F (37 °C), the average body temperature

Did you find the truth?

T At Thanksgiving, there is a hotline that explains how to cook a turkey safely.

F All bacteria are bad for your body.

Resources

Books

Rue, Nancy R. and Anna Graf Williams. *Quick Reference to Food Safety and Sanitation*. Upper Saddle River, NJ: Prentice Hall, 2002.

Ruffin, Frances E. *Kitchen Smarts: Food Safety and Kitchen Equipment*. New York: Rosen Publishing Group, 2005.

Schlosser, Eric, and Charles Wilson. *Chew on This: Everything You Don't Want to Know About Fast Food*. New York: Houghton Mifflin, 2006.

Sherrow, Victoria. *Food Safety*. New York: Chelsea House Publications, 2007.

Snedden, Robert. *The Benefits of Bacteria*. Portsmouth, NH: Heinemann, 2007.

Taylor-Butler, Christine. *Food Allergies* (A True Book™: Health and the Human Body). New York: Children's Press, 2008.

Taylor-Butler, Christine. *The Food Pyramid* (A True Book™: Health and the Human Body). New York: Children's Press, 2008.

Organizations and Web Sites

Fight BAC!
www.fightbac.org
Learn food safety in four simple steps.

Food Safe Schools
www.foodsafeschools.org
This Web site has information about food safety in schools.

FDA Center for Food Safety and Applied Nutrition
www.cfsan.fda.gov/~dms/educate.html
This site includes food-safety puzzles, quizzes, and tips for writing a school report.

Place to Visit

Centers for Disease Control and Prevention (CDC)
1600 Clifton Road
Atlanta, GA 30333
404-639-0830
www.cdc.gov/about/resources/visit.htm
Experience a multimedia installation about health sciences and the history of the CDC.

Important Words

bacteria (bak-TIHR-ee-uh) – tiny, one-celled living things. Some bacteria cause disease.

contaminate – to make dirty, poisonous, or unfit for use

diarrhea (dye-uh-REE-uh) – a condition in which feces leave the body frequently in liquid form

disinfectant – a type of cleaning solution that can kill microbes

microbe (MYE-krobe) – a tiny living thing, such as a virus or bacteria, that is too small to be seen without a microscope

mold – a fungus that grows on food and damp things

organic (or-GAN-ik) – produced using only natural products rather than chemically formulated products, such as pesticides

pasteurization (pass-chuh-rih-ZAY-shuhn) – a heat treatment used to kill bacteria in foods such as milk

pesticide – a chemical used to kill insects and other organisms harmful to plants

quarantine (KWOR-uhn-teen) – the isolation of a person or an animal to prevent the spread of a disease

Index

Page numbers in **bold** indicate illustrations

About the Author

Christine Taylor-Butler lives in Kansas City, Missouri, with her husband and two daughters. A native of Ohio, she is the author of more than 40 books for children. She holds a B.S. degree in both Civil Engineering and Art and Design from the Massachusetts Institute of Technology in Cambridge, MA. Other books by Ms. Taylor-Butler in the True Book Health and the Human Body series include: *The Food Pyramid*, *Food Allergies*, *The Circulatory System*, *The Respiratory System*, *The Digestive System*, and *The Nervous System*.

PHOTOGRAPHS: Big Stock Photo (p. 8; fruit salad, cream pie, p. 9; moldy oranges, p. 11; peas, p. 17); www.fightbac.org (p. 33); Getty Images (food cover with fly, cover; p. 12; p. 15; pp. 26–27; p. 42); iStockPhoto.com (frosted cup cakes, cover; pp. 3–5; coleslaw, mustard, p. 9; moldy sandwich, p. 11; p. 13; p. 16; egg tray, p. 17; p. 20; cans, p. 21; p. 24; milk, p. 30; pp. 34–35; p. 37; p. 41; p. 43; Alex Bramwell, p. 32; Anne Clark, p. 6); Masterfile (p. 39); Photodisc (p. 21); Photolibrary (p. 23; p. 36; p. 40); Stockxpert (back cover); Tranz/Corbis (p. 10; p. 14; p. 18; p. 22; p. 25; p. 28; p. 31). All other images property of Weldon Owen Education.